BEING WITH GOD

A Bible and prayer guide
for people with dementia

WORDS OF
PEACE

Also in the **Being with God** series: *Words of hope, Words of faith.*

Copyright © Scripture Union 2010

ISBN: 9781844275229

Scripture Union, 207–209 Queensway, Bletchley,
Milton Keynes, MK2 2EB, England
Email: info@scriptureunion.org.uk
Website: www.scriptureunion.org.uk

Scripture Union USA, PO Box 987, Valley Forge, PA 19482, USA
Email: info@scriptureunion.org
Website: www.scriptureunion.org

Scripture Union Australia, Locked Bag 2, Central Coast Business Centre,
NSW 2252, Australia
Website: www.scriptureunion.org.au

Scripture quotations, unless otherwise indicated, are taken from the HOLY BIBLE,
NEW INTERNATIONAL VERSION. Copyright © 1973, 1978, 1984 by International
Bible Society. Anglicisation copyright © 1979, 1984, 1989, 1995, 1996, 2001.
Used by permission of Hodder & Stoughton Ltd.

British Library Cataloguing-in-Publication Data: a catalogue record of this book
is available from the British Library.

Developed and edited by 'Tricia Williams
Expert consultant and introduction: Margaret Goodall
All recordings produced by Gordon Lorenz

Cover design and internal layout by Martin Lore
Printed and bound in Singapore by Tien Wah Press Ltd

Scripture Union is an international Christian charity working with churches
in more than 130 countries providing resources to bring the good news of Jesus
Christ to children, young people and families and to encourage them to develop
spiritually through the Bible and prayer. As well as coordinating a network of
volunteers, staff and associates who run holidays, church-based events and school
Christian groups, Scripture Union produces a wide range of publications and
supports those who use their resources through training programmes.

'DRAW NIGH TO GOD,
AND HE WILL
DRAW NIGH TO YOU.'

James 4:8, KJV

FOR MARY AND SHEILA

CONTENTS

FOREWORD

Dementia is a cruel robber. It robs people of their memory, their personality, their ability to recognise and react normally even with partners and family they've loved for years. In short, it robs them of themselves and the life they've known. Confusion and strangeness replace the familiar and safe. They have a whole lifetime of experience and knowledge behind them – yet that knowledge is tantalisingly beyond their mind's grasp.

The knowledge which escapes them may well include a lifelong faith in God and a love of his word in the Bible which has been a constant source of strength and reassurance during challenging times in the past. However, with the onset of dementia, that comfort is lost to them as much-loved biblical stories, prayers and hymns are frustratingly hard to remember.

With its carefully chosen mix of familiar words and evocative music, this imaginative and practical resource is nothing less than a Godsend – a nudge to the memory which at its most obvious level is a delightful way to aid conversation and recall, but at its deepest, opens, for the person with dementia, a real connection to faith and the God who has never stopped loving them.

Pam Rhodes
Presenter of BBC's Songs of Praise,
Patron of Methodist Homes for the Aged

WELCOME
AND THANKS

We hope that you will find this Bible and prayer guide brings you God's blessing and comfort – whether you are the person with dementia or you are a 'carer'.

This resource has been developed specifically for people with dementia, but older people who are struggling with memory loss may also find it helpful.

We are so grateful for the help and encouragement of many in the creation of this resource. **Margaret Goodall**, Chaplaincy Advisor for **MHA**, has given constant encouragement as our expert consultant. We've also much appreciated help and advice from **Christian Council on Ageing** and **Alzheimer's Society**. Individuals facing the challenges of dementia have given invaluable feedback on the content. We are especially grateful for the support and encouragement of **Pam Rhodes**, presenter of BBC's **Songs of Praise**, Patron of MHA.

Our thanks too to all those who have given towards the development of these resources – including: MHA, Christian Council on Ageing and Social Interface Ltd – whose generosity has helped enormously in the creation of this resource.

Words of peace: the CD

With its familiar hymns and evocative performances, this CD has been specially produced and compiled for inclusion in this guide. It would not have been possible without the generous support of Gordon Lorenz, music producer, and of the professional and highly gifted performers he has brought together. Our thanks to all of those who have been involved in these recordings, and for their great creativity and sensitivity in bringing us this music.

Our prayer is that – as you use this guide – you will know that God is close to you, as you draw near to him.

'Tricia Williams
Editor

INTRODUCTION

A WORD FOR CARERS

Some older people, either because they are living with dementia or because of age, are no longer able to join in public worship. The following pages offer a way to help them reconnect with the Christian faith and story.

People with dementia are sometimes thought of as no longer being able to worship. But even when people have not spoken for a while – as those involved in their care will know – they are still able to join in with familiar prayers and hymns. We need to offer clues as to what is going on, a context for worship, and cues in the words that are so familiar, in order to help them join in.

As the effects of dementia increase, it is more difficult to interact with others and to be understood. But while thoughts and words may be confused, feelings and emotions experienced are still real. So if we can meet people on an emotional or 'feeling' level instead of the rational or thinking level, then we meet people who are like us but who need help to be part of the world around them.

I hope that by using this Bible and prayer guide, people who could be isolated by dementia, will be helped to feel once again part of the Christian community, and be reminded that God loves and accepts them as they are – something we all need reminding of.

We believe in a God who can reach beyond our reasoning and understanding of words to touch us again with his love.

Margaret Goodall
Chaplaincy Advisor, MHA

HOW TO USE
THIS GUIDE

SETTING THE SCENE

In order to use this Bible and prayer guide to best effect it will be important to 'set the scene' so that the person with dementia can recognise what is going to happen. Imagine what it's like to wake up in a strange place. For a moment all is odd and 'wrong'. For those with dementia it is always like this. So, as carers, we need to do all we can to help them focus.

Using the same setting each time we use this guide can help provide a way of 'cueing in' and be a reminder of what is about to take place. For example, a small table, with a white cloth and a Bible, cross or prayer book could make any room into the place where we regularly take time to 'be with God'. If possible, use the same Bible each time.

The same words used to introduce the session could become a familiar part of this time and again provide a cue into worship. The words need to be simple and easy to remember, affirming God's presence. For example:

God is here
God is always here

God is with us
God is always with us

EACH DAY'S DEVOTIONAL

Each day's devotional follows a regular format which it is hoped, for some, may become a familiar prompt for this special time with God. We understand that each person with dementia (or elderly person struggling with memory loss) is an individual and will be at different stages in facing the challenges of dementia or age. For this reason, the devotionals aren't intended to be scripts. Feel free to take the suggestions here and use what is helpful or let them act as springboards to ideas and words which will help you 'come near to God' in your particular situation. Each day's outline includes:

Prayer
The prayer at the beginning picks up on one of the themes in the Bible verses. If thanks or prayer needs are mentioned, you might like to add specific things which are known to you and relevant to your particular situation. If helpful, encourage the person you are with to join in saying the 'Amen' at the end of the prayer.

Read
Try to use the same Bible every time you use these devotionals. If possible, choose one that the person with dementia is familiar with. It's hoped that the Bible and this booklet will be helpful cues for this time.

You might choose to use the whole Bible passage given or just the verse selection printed – whichever is easiest or most appropriate for your situation.

Talk about…

This section aims to start you thinking and talking about the Bible verses. It picks up words and ideas from the Bible passage to prompt thinking about the themes in ways which might help bring a sense of God's presence. Choose ideas that are appropriate and helpful in your situation.

Pray

You may like to say the Lord's Prayer each time you use one of these daily devotionals. It will probably have been familiar to many people and they may enjoy saying it aloud. It might be useful to use a traditional form of the prayer, for example:

Our Father, which art in heaven,
Hallowed be thy Name,
Thy kingdom come,
Thy will be done on earth as it is in heaven.
Give us this day our daily bread;
And forgive us our trespasses,
   as we forgive those who trespass against us;
And lead us not into temptation
   but deliver us from evil.
For thine is the kingdom, the power and
   the glory,
   forever and ever. Amen.

Hymn or song

You might like to sing together a favourite hymn of your own choice, or listen to the suggested track from the CD – created especially for this resource – included at the back of this volume.

The CD with its wide range of music – choral, brass band, children's choirs, a gospel group and soloists – has a hymn or song (or even a chorus from Sunday school days!) which links in with the theme of each day's Bible verses. You could sing along, or invite others to come and sing with you. However you choose to use it, we hope that these evocative recordings will bring God's comfort to those using this material.

Cues and clues box

The various suggestions are intended to act as cues and clues to the ideas and themes of the Bible verses. You might like to look at a picture, hold an object, listen to music or even paint in response to the day's devotional. Choose or adapt as most appropriate to the person with dementia, or older person, using this Bible and prayer guide.

DAILY BIBLE
READINGS

IN THE BEGINNING, GOD…

1   'In the beginning God…'
    Genesis 1:1,31
2   'The LORD bless you…'
    Numbers 6:22–27
3   'Love the LORD your God…'
    Deuteronomy 6:1–9
4   'Be strong and courageous…'
    Joshua 1:6–9
5   'I know that my Redeemer lives'
    Job 19:25–27
6   'For unto us a child is born'
    Isaiah 9:2,6,7
7   'Comfort, comfort my people…'
    Isaiah 40:1–5
8   'Fear not, for I have
    redeemed you…'
    Isaiah 43:1–7
9   'Surely he took our infirmities…'
    Isaiah 53:1–6
10 'Call to me…'
    Jeremiah 33:2,3
11 '…to walk humbly with your God'
    Micah 6:8

PEACE – THROUGH JESUS

12 The day of Pentecost
    Acts 2:1–4
13 Peter heals a lame man
    Acts 3:1–10
14 Peace and joy through Jesus
    Romans 5:1–5
15 *Abba*, Father
    Romans 8:15–17

16 Nothing can separate us
    from God's love
    Romans 8:37–39
17 The Lord's Supper
    1 Corinthians 11:23–26
18 Love is…
    1 Corinthians 13:4–13
19 The fruit of the Spirit
    Galatians 5:22–25
20 Spiritual blessings in Christ
    Ephesians 1:3–8
21 The armour of God
    Ephesians 6:10–18
22 At the name of Jesus
    Philippians 2:5–11
23 The peace of Christ
    Colossians 3:12–17
24 'Be joyful always…'
    1 Thessalonians 5:16–24
25 'Let us fix our eyes on Jesus…'
    Hebrews 12:1–3
26 The prayer of faith
    James 5:13–16
27 God's love
    1 John 4:7–12
28 'To him who is able…'
    Jude 24,25
29 'Here I am…'
    Revelation 3:20
30 No more crying…
    Revelation 21:1–4
31 The river of life
    Revelation 22:1–5

IN THE
BEGINNING, GOD...

Enjoy these words of blessing
and encouragement from the Old
Testament; let them bring you God's
comfort and peace as you hear his
words and promises.

'IN THE
BEGINNING GOD...'

PRAYER
Praise you, heavenly Father, for the beauty of
your creation. Thank you for your good world.
Amen.

READING Genesis 1:1,31

**In the beginning God created the heavens and
the earth. ... God saw all that he had made, and
it was very good.**
Genesis 1:1,31

TALK ABOUT...
☐ The beauty of creation (an aspect that you
  particularly enjoy)
☐ Country walks; holiday places;
  people you know
☐ Good and beautiful things in your life
☐ God made a good and beautiful world
☐ Thank God for the beauty of his creation

PRAY
'Our Father, which art in heaven...'

HYMN OR SONG
'How great thou art'
(CD, *Words of peace*, track 1)

'THE LORD BLESS YOU...'

Pictures

Photos of special times; kind, friendly faces; people you know and love.

Objects

A card with the words of Numbers 6:24–26 to keep close to you through today.

To do

Say the words (or just the first phrase) of Numbers 6:24–26 to each other – with an arm around shoulders if appropriate.

PRAYER

Lord God, thank you for being with us.
Please fill us with your peace now. *Amen.*

READING Numbers 6:22–27

The LORD bless you and keep you; the LORD make his face shine upon you and be gracious to you; the LORD turn his face towards you and give you peace.
Numbers 6:24–26

TALK ABOUT...
☐ Kind faces; people being kind to you and helping you
☐ Times and places where you feel peaceful
☐ Times when God has been good to you

PRAY
'Our Father, which art in heaven...'

HYMN OR SONG
'Count your blessings'
(CD, *Words of peace,* track 2)

'LOVE THE LORD YOUR GOD...'

CUES AND CLUES

Some of the following might help as you read today's verses from the Bible and pray.

Pictures
Rule books; the Ten Commandments – any fine art or Bible storybook image of the tablets of stone, or of Moses bringing these down from the mountain; a Bible.

Objects
Any physical clue to rules and God's commandments (eg a familiar tapestry with the Ten Commandments); a Bible; a cross.

To do
If easy to arrange, you may even like to watch a relevant clip from the film *The Ten Commandments* (1956) with Charlton Heston (directed by Cecil B DeMille).

PRAYER
Lord God, help us to love and serve you in everything we do and say today. *Amen.*

READING Deuteronomy 6:1–9

Love the LORD your God with all your heart and with all your soul and with all your strength.
Deuteronomy 6:5

TALK ABOUT...
☐ Rules; God's rules; the Bible
☐ The Ten Commandments (Deuteronomy 5:1–21; Exodus 20:1–17)
☐ Reminiscences of times and places where you first heard the Ten Commandments (eg Sunday school; school assemblies; at home as a child)
☐ How we show our love to God

PRAY
'Our Father, which art in heaven...'

HYMN OR SONG
'Trust and obey'
(CD, *Words of peace*, track 3)

'BE STRONG AND COURAGEOUS...'

CUES AND CLUES

Some of the following might help as you read today's verses from the Bible and pray.

Pictures
Wartime photos; mountain climbers; an adult holding a child's hand as they walk or do something difficult; a parent holding a baby.

Objects
Small training weights; a medal (for bravery) – this might be a war medal, a badge or award, a rosette.

To do
If appropriate, put your arm around the shoulder of the person with whom you are reading and praying.

PRAYER
Lord God, help us to be strong and courageous. Thank you that you are with us now. *Amen.*

READING Joshua 1:6–9

Be strong and courageous. Do not be terrified; do not be discouraged, for the LORD your God will be with wherever you go.
Joshua 1:9

TALK ABOUT...
☐ Strength; training to build up strength (eg weight-training)
☐ Acts of courage and bravery; stories of courage (eg wartime acts of bravery)
☐ A time when you've been scared; worries
☐ God is with us – wherever we are

PRAY
'Our Father, which art in heaven...'

HYMN OR SONG
'He who would valiant be'
(CD, *Words of peace*, track 4)

'I KNOW THAT MY REDEEMER LIVES'

PRAYER

Lord God, my Redeemer, praise you for the everlasting hope we have in you – whatever the struggles and difficulties we face today. *Amen.*

READING Job 19:25–27

I know that my Redeemer lives, and that in the end he will stand upon the earth.
Job 19:25

TALK ABOUT...

☐ Illness – your own or of those close to you; memories of times of ill-health
☐ The meaning of 'Redeemer' and related ideas (eg a pawn broker's; *Green Shield* stamps; talk about someone's redeeming features)
☐ Jesus is alive and knows our situation – we are safe with him

PRAY

'Our Father, which art in heaven...'

HYMN OR SONG

'Up from the grave he arose'
(CD, *Words of peace*, track 5)

'FOR UNTO US A CHILD IS BORN'

Some of the following might help as you read today's verses from the Bible and pray.

Pictures
The Light of theWorld by Holman Hunt; a nativity scene (eg a Christmas card) focusing on the baby Jesus.

Objects
A lighted candle; a cross.

Music
'For unto us a child is born' (chorus from Handel's *Messiah*).

PRAYER
Father God, thank you for sending Jesus into our world. Thank you for bringing us your peace now. *Amen.*

READING Isaiah 9:2,6,7

For to us a child is born, to us a son is given, and the government will be on his shoulders. And he will be called Wonderful Counsellor, Mighty God, Everlasting Father, Prince of Peace.
Isaiah 9:6

TALK ABOUT...
☐ Lights – in the night; power cuts; when it's dark, city lights (see v 2)
☐ Babies, young children
☐ Jesus coming into our world as a baby; Christmas
☐ God is our Father; Jesus – the Prince of Peace – brings us peace

PRAY
'Our Father, which art in heaven…'

HYMN OR SONG
'Silent night, holy night'
(CD, *Words of peace*, track 6)

'COMFORT, COMFORT MY PEOPLE...'

CUES AND CLUES

Some of the following might help as you read today's verses from the Bible and pray.

Pictures
A parent comforting a child; a photo of Jerusalem; a cross; mountains, valleys or desert (vs 3,4).

Objects
A warm scarf or something comforting to hold; a cross.

Music
'Comfort ye' from Handel's *Messiah*.

PRAYER
Lord God, please bring us your comfort as we listen to your word now. Come near to us as we draw near to you. *Amen.*

READING Isaiah 40:1–5

Comfort, comfort my people, says your God. Speak tenderly to Jerusalem, and proclaim to her that her hard service has been completed, that her sin has been paid for, that she has received from the Lord's hand double for all her sins.
Isaiah 40:1,2

TALK ABOUT...
☐ Comforting a child after an upset
☐ Rest after hard work
☐ A long, hard journey (vs 3,4)
☐ Preparing for a very special visit from a long-awaited friend
☐ God offers us forgiveness for all our sins through Jesus
☐ God comes to his people

PRAY
'Our Father, which art in heaven...'

HYMN OR SONG
'O worship the Lord in the beauty of holiness' (CD, *Words of peace*, track 7)

'FEAR NOT, FOR I HAVE REDEEMED YOU...'

PRAYER
Lord God, thank you that you know each of us by name. Thank you for loving us and for protecting us. *Amen.*

READING Isaiah 43:1–7

Fear not, for I have redeemed you; I have summoned you by name; you are mine. When you pass through the ... rivers, they will not sweep over you.
Isaiah 43:1,2

TALK ABOUT...
☐ Things that make us afraid
☐ Your name; why you were given that name
☐ Rivers; a river that is familiar to you
☐ God protects us and cares for us in difficult times

PRAY
'Our Father, which art in heaven...'

HYMN OR SONG
'Be still my soul'
(CD, *Words of peace*, track 8)

'SURELY HE TOOK OUR INFIRMITIES...'

CUES AND CLUES

Some of the following might help as you read today's verses from the Bible and pray.

Pictures
Sheep in a field; Jesus on the cross.

Objects
A 'toy' sheep to hold; a cross.

PRAYER
Lord Jesus, thank you for taking our sorrows and sins when you died on the cross. *Amen.*

READING Isaiah 53:1–6

Surely he took our infirmities and carried our sorrows ...
Isaiah 53:4

TALK ABOUT...
☐ Sheep – and their behaviour
☐ God gave his Son, Jesus, for us
☐ Jesus is with us and wants to carry our load
☐ We can be sure of God's forgiveness and that he is close to us

PRAY
'Our Father, which art in heaven...'

HYMN OR SONG
'The old rugged cross'
(CD, *Words of peace,* track 9)

'CALL TO ME...'

PRAYER

Thank you, Lord God, that you know what is in
our hearts even when we can't put our thoughts
and feelings into words. Please hear us now.
Amen.

READING Jeremiah 33:2,3

**Call to me and I will answer you and
tell you great and unsearchable things you
do not know.**
Jeremiah 33:3

TALK ABOUT...

☐ Telephone calls
☐ Answers to prayer; other people's stories
of answered prayer
☐ We can speak to God and he is listening

PRAY

'Our Father, which art in heaven...'

HYMN OR SONG

'What a friend we have in Jesus'
(CD, *Words of peace*, track 10)

'...TO WALK HUMBLY WITH YOUR GOD'

CUES AND CLUES

Some of the following might help as you read today's verses from the Bible and pray.

Pictures
Friends on a walk together; a pathway; taking a dog for a walk.

Objects
A walking stick; walking boots.

PRAYER
Lord God, please help us to walk with you today and to know that you are close by our side. *Amen.*

READING Micah 6:8

And what does the Lord require of you? To act justly and to love mercy and to walk humbly with your God.
Micah 6:8

TALK ABOUT...
☐ Reminiscences about instances of kindness and fairness
☐ Going for a walk with a good friend
☐ God is with us as we walk through life today

PRAY
'Our Father, which art in heaven...'

HYMN OR SONG
'Just a closer walk with thee'
(CD, *Words of peace*, track 11)

PEACE –
THROUGH JESUS

May the peace of God which comes
to us through Jesus keep you as you read
these words from Acts and the letters
of the New Testament.

THE DAY OF PENTECOST

PRAYER
Holy Spirit, come close to us now and fill us with a sense of your presence. *Amen.*

READING Acts 2:1–4

When the day of Pentecost came, they were all together in one place. Suddenly a sound like the blowing of a violent wind came from heaven and filled the whole house where they were sitting. They saw what seemed to be tongues of fire that separated and came to rest on each of them. All of them were filled with the Holy Spirit and began to speak in other tongues as the Spirit enabled them.
Acts 2:1–4

TALK ABOUT…
- ☐ Experiences of strong winds and gales; fire and flames
- ☐ Times when the Holy Spirit has seemed close to you
- ☐ God the Holy Spirit is with us now

PRAY
'Our Father, which art in heaven…'

HYMN OR SONG
'Breathe on me breath of God'
(CD, *Words of peace*, track 12)

PETER HEALS A LAME MAN

CUES AND CLUES

Some of the following might help as you read today's verses from the Bible and pray.

Pictures
Photos of happy celebrations – your birthday or Christmas parties.

Objects
A piece of celebration cake; streamers to suggest celebration.

To do
If there's been a birthday or anniversary involving people you know, you could bring along cards, balloons etc – and share some celebration food.

PRAYER

Lord Jesus, we thank you for your help today and for the good things you bring into our lives. *Amen.*

READING Acts 3:1–10

Then Peter said, 'Silver or gold I do not have, but what I have I give you. In the name of Jesus Christ of Nazareth, walk.' … He jumped to his feet and began to walk. Then he went with them into the temple courts, walking and jumping, and praising God.
Acts 3:6,8

TALK ABOUT…

☐ Surprises – the man didn't expect to be healed
☐ This story – the man being healed and then jumping for joy
☐ What God has given you or done for you that you want to thank and praise him for
☐ Celebrations for good things that happen
☐ God wants to help you

PRAY

'Our Father, which art in heaven…'

HYMN OR SONG

'Praise to the Holiest in the height'
(CD, *Words of peace*, track 13)

PEACE AND JOY THROUGH JESUS

PRAYER
Lord Jesus, thank you for your peace and joy. Help us to know the peace of your presence with us now. *Amen.*

READING Romans 5:1–5

Therefore, since we have been justified through faith, we have peace with God through our Lord Jesus Christ ... And we rejoice in the hope of the glory of God.
Romans 5:1,2

TALK ABOUT...
☐ Peace: places that you find peaceful (eg gardens, mountains, church)
☐ Things that make you feel happy and joyful
☐ God gives us his peace and joy

PRAY
'Our Father, which art in heaven…'

HYMN OR SONG
'Blessed assurance, Jesus is mine'
(CD, *Words of peace*, track 14)

ABBA, FATHER

Some of the following might help as you read today's verses from the Bible and pray.

Pictures
Photos of your family when you were a child – try to find some old photos; pictures of the prodigal son being welcomed home by his father (eg *The Return of the Prodigal Son* by Rembrandt).

Objects
Father's Day cards (if these will prompt positive feelings).

PRAYER
Lord God, thank you that you are our Father and we are your children. Thank you that you are always ready to welcome us. *Amen.*

READING Romans 8:15–17

For you did not receive a spirit that makes you a slave again to fear, but you received the Spirit of sonship. And by him we cry, 'Abba, Father.' The Spirit himself testifies with our spirit that we are God's children.
Romans 8:15, 16

TALK ABOUT...
☐ Families
☐ Childhood reminiscences
☐ God is our Father – the best Father

PRAY
'Our Father, which art in heaven...'

HYMN OR SONG
'Dear Lord and Father of mankind'
(CD, *Words of peace*, track 15)

NOTHING CAN SEPARATE US FROM GOD'S LOVE

Some of the following
might help as you read
today's verses from the
Bible and pray.

Pictures
Mountains; the Grand
Canyon; wide rivers;
photos of family.

To do
If you know the old
chorus 'Wide, wide
as the ocean' (from
Sunday school days),
you might enjoy singing
this together and doing
the 'actions' to celebrate
God's love for you.

PRAYER
Lord God, thank you that nothing can separate us from your love. *Amen.*

READING Romans 8:37–39

For I am convinced that neither death nor life, neither angels nor demons, neither the present nor the future, nor any powers, neither height nor depth, nor anything else in all creation, will be able to separate us from the love of God that is in Christ Jesus our Lord. *Romans 8:38,39*

TALK ABOUT...
☐ Mountains, deep valleys, wide rivers – things that separate
☐ Your 'loved ones'
☐ Nothing can separate us from God's love

PRAY
'Our Father, which art in heaven…'

HYMN OR SONG
'O Love that wilt not let me go'
(CD, *Words of peace*, track 16)

17

THE LORD'S SUPPER

CUES AND CLUES

Some of the following might help as you read today's verses from the Bible and pray.

Pictures
The Last Supper (fine art pictures, eg by Leonardo da Vinci); bread and wine; celebratory meals with others.

Objects
Fresh bread; 'wine' (non-alcoholic).

To do
Break the bread, smell the freshness; share and eat some bread; if appropriate, you may like to attend or receive communion together.

PRAYER
Lord Jesus, we praise you for giving your life for us. Help us to think of you as we read your word and pray now. *Amen.*

READING 1 Corinthians 11:23–26

For I received from the Lord what I also passed on to you: The Lord Jesus, on the night he was betrayed, took bread, and when he had given thanks, he broke it and said, 'This is my body, which is for you; do this in remembrance of me.'
1 Corinthians 11:23,24

TALK ABOUT…
☐ Meals you enjoy; food and celebration
☐ Bread – different kinds, what you like about bread
☐ The Lord's Supper, or 'Communion', at church
☐ Bread – as a prompt to thinking about Jesus and his life given for us

PRAY
'Jesus, keep me near the cross'

HYMN OR SONG
'Sweet is the work, my God, my King'
(CD, *Words of peace*, track 17)

LOVE IS...

Some of the following might help as you read today's verses from the Bible and pray.

Pictures
Find pictures which illustrate different kinds of love: mother and baby, parents and child, friends and carers, wedding pictures (eg if you're married, photos of your wedding).

Objects
A romantic 'heart' (eg a cushion); a wedding ring.

To do
...or have with you a much-loved pet.

PRAYER
Lord Jesus, please may we know your loving arms around us. Please help us to show and share your love with others. *Amen.*

READING 1 Corinthians 13:4–13

Love is patient, love is kind. .... Love does not delight in evil but rejoices with the truth. It always protects, always trusts, always hopes, always perseveres. .... And now these three remain: faith, hope and love. But the greatest of these is love.
1 Corinthians 13:4,6,7,13

TALK ABOUT...
- ☐ Love – experiences of being loved and loving (eg parents and children; being 'in love')
- ☐ Being patient and kind; persevering
- ☐ Acts of kindness and love from those around us (eg family, carers)
- ☐ God loves us like this – and showed his love to us in Jesus
- ☐ God wants us to share his love

PRAY
'Our Father, which art in heaven...'

HYMN OR SONG
'Love divine, all loves excelling'
(CD, *Words of peace*, track 18)

19

THE FRUIT
OF THE SPIRIT

CUES AND CLUES

Some of the following
might help as you read
today's verses from the
Bible and pray.

Pictures
A beautiful fruit tree.

Objects
A piece of fruit.

To do
Eat the fruit (taste, smell,
enjoy), if you'd like to.

PRAYER
Holy Spirit, we praise you that you are with us.
Grow in us the fruit of your Spirit. *Amen.*

READING Galatians 5:22–25

**But the fruit of the Spirit is love, joy, peace,
patience, kindness, goodness, faithfulness,
gentleness and self-control.**
Galatians 5:22,23

TALK ABOUT...
☐ Favourite fruit (the look, the smell, the taste)
and fruit trees (eg apples or plums on a tree)
☐ The fruit that God gives us and thankfulness
for these (eg loving relationships, feelings
and times of joy, peace)
☐ God wants to help us to be loving and
kind to others too

PRAY
'Our Father, which art in heaven…'

HYMN OR SONG
'Give me joy in my heart…'
(CD, *Words of peace*, track 19)

SPIRITUAL BLESSINGS IN CHRIST

CUES AND CLUES

Some of the following might help as you read today's verses from the Bible and pray.

Pictures
Good things which prompt praise and thanks to God; a congregation singing; a cross.

Objects
Simple percussion instruments, music, an instrument you have played; a small cross to hold.

To do
You might like to use one of the instruments as you listen to or sing the hymn.

PRAYER
Praise God for all you give to us through your Son, Jesus. *Amen.*

READING Ephesians 1:3–8

Praise be to the God and Father of our Lord Jesus Christ, who has blessed us in the heavenly realms with every spiritual blessing in Christ.
Ephesians 1:3

TALK ABOUT...
☐ Things that make us happy
☐ Thanking God for all he gives us – practically, but also in Christ Jesus
☐ Times of praising God (eg at church, reminiscences about other situations)

PRAY
'Our Father, which art in heaven…'

HYMN OR SONG
'A wonderful Saviour is Jesus my Lord'
(CD, *Words of peace*, track 20)

THE ARMOUR OF GOD

CUES AND CLUES

Some of the following might help as you read today's verses from the Bible and pray.

Pictures
Armour: sword, shield, helmet etc; praying hands (eg the picture by Albrecht Dürer).

Objects
A helmet (eg a cycle helmet) or shield.

PRAYER
Lord God, help us to be strong in you.
Please increase our faith and help us to trust in you. *Amen.*

READING Ephesians 6:10–18

Finally, be strong in the Lord and in his mighty power. Put on the full armour of God ... Stand firm then ... with the breastplate of righteousness in place ... take up the shield of faith ... Take the helmet of salvation and the sword of the Spirit, which is the word of God.
Ephesians 6:10,11,14,16,17

TALK ABOUT...
- ☐ Reminiscences about armour (swords, shields, helmets etc – museums, history books)
- ☐ Stories of faith and answers to prayers
- ☐ We are safe in the arms of Jesus
- ☐ God gives us his strength to face whatever this day brings

PRAY
'Our Father, which art in heaven...'

HYMN OR SONG
'Fight the good fight'
(CD, *Words of peace*, track 21)

AT THE NAME
OF JESUS

PRAYER
Lord Jesus, thank you that even though you are a
king, you came to earth to serve us. *Amen.*

READING Philippians 2:5–11

**Your attitude should be the same as that of
Christ Jesus: Who, being in very nature God,
did not consider equality with God something
to be grasped, but made himself nothing,
taking the very nature of a servant, being made
in human likeness.**
Philippians 2:5–7

TALK ABOUT...
- ☐ Servants and kings (or queen) –
  any experiences of either
- ☐ The name of 'Jesus' – what it means to you
- ☐ Even though Jesus is 'King of kings',
  he came to serve people
- ☐ What it might mean for you to serve others
- ☐ Honouring Jesus – and how we do that
  in our daily lives

PRAY
'Our Father, which art in heaven...'

HYMN OR SONG
'All hail the power of Jesus' name'
(CD, *Words of peace*, track 22)

THE PEACE
OF CHRIST

CUES AND CLUES

Some of the following
might help as you read
today's verses from the
Bible and pray.

Pictures
Peaceful places –
especially ones which
might be familiar.

To do
Rest quietly and listen
to the hymn 'Jesus is the
sweetest name I know'.

PRAYER
Lord Jesus, may your peace rule in our hearts
today. We thank you for all the good things you
give to us. *Amen.*

READING Colossians 3:12–17

**Let the peace of Christ rule in your hearts,
since as members of one body you were called
to peace. And be thankful.**
Colossians 3:15

TALK ABOUT…
☐ Peaceful situations you enjoy (eg a place,
   a time of day, people)
☐ People and things you enjoy (eg a view
   from a window, a garden, a meal you enjoy,
   a kind carer, an amusing TV programme,
   favourite music)
☐ Jesus is with you and wants to give you
   his peace

PRAY
'Our Father, which art in heaven…'

HYMN OR SONG
'Jesus is the sweetest name I know'
(CD, *Words of peace,* track 23)

'BE JOYFUL ALWAYS...'

CUES AND CLUES

Some of the following might help as you read today's verses from the Bible and pray.

Pictures
Children or older people smiling and laughing; people praising God in church.

Objects
A 'thank you' card; some simple musical instruments; a book of prayers.

To do
You might like to sing along to the song, 'O happy day'.

PRAYER
Lord Jesus, fill us with your joy today. We thank and praise you for all you give us. *Amen.*

READING 1 Thessalonians 5:16–24

Be joyful always; pray continually; give thanks in all circumstances, for this is God's will for you in Christ Jesus.
1 Thessalonians 5:16–18

TALK ABOUT...
☐ Things that give us joy; things for which we are thankful
☐ What makes you cheerful
☐ God gives us his joy and peace
☐ We're safe with God and can rely on him

PRAY
'Our Father, which art in heaven...'

HYMN OR SONG
'O happy day'
(CD, *Words of peace*, track 24)

'LET US FIX OUR EYES ON JESUS...'

CUES AND CLUES

Some of the following might help as you read today's verses from the Bible and pray.

Pictures

School sports days; running races; the finishing line.

Objects

Running shoes; a finishing tape; a winner's medal.

PRAYER

Father God, when we're finding it difficult to keep going, help us look to Jesus. *Amen.*

READING Hebrews 12:1–3

...let us run with perseverance the race marked out for us. Let us fix our eyes on Jesus, the author and perfecter of our faith ... Consider him who endured such opposition from sinful men, so that you will not grow weary and lose heart.

Hebrews 12:1–3

TALK ABOUT...

☐ Running races, school sports days
  (eg trying to win, winning and losing)
☐ Feeling sad and tired
☐ Fix your eyes on Jesus
☐ God knows all about us
☐ He understands how we feel and will
  help us keep going

PRAY

'Our Father, which art in heaven...'

HYMN OR SONG

'Turn your eyes upon Jesus'
(CD, *Words of peace*, track 25)

THE PRAYER
OF FAITH

CUES AND CLUES

Some of the following might help as you read today's verses from the Bible and pray.

Pictures
People at prayer.

Objects
If this is part of your church tradition, a 'kneeler' to suggest prayer.

To do
If comfortable with this idea, you could pray for each other, thinking of the troubles and joys that have been mentioned.

PRAYER
Lord God, please hear and answer us as we pray today. *Amen.*

READING James 5:13–16

Is any one of you in trouble? He should pray. Is anyone happy? Let him sing songs of praise. Is any one of you sick? He should call the elders of the church to pray over him … The prayer of a righteous man is powerful and effective.
James 5:13,14,16

TALK ABOUT…
☐ Talk about troubles, things that make you happy, health problems
☐ God hears us when we pray and will answer (not always in the way we think he might!)

PRAY
'Our Father, which art in heaven…'

HYMN OR SONG
'Read your Bible, pray every day'
(CD, *Words of peace,* track 26)

GOD'S LOVE

CUES AND CLUES

Some of the following might help as you read today's verses from the Bible and pray.

Pictures
Photos of you with family or friends; wedding photos; pictures of Jesus with children (eg from Bible storybooks).

Objects
A simple cross to hold.

To do
Share some fruit, biscuits or chocolates as a sign of sharing God's love with others.

PRAYER

Lord God, thank you for your love shown to us through your Son, Jesus. Help us to share your love with others. *Amen.*

READING 1 John 4:7–12

Dear friends, let us love one another, for love comes from God.
1 John 4:7

TALK ABOUT...

☐ People you love; people who love you
☐ Sharing God's love with other people in the way we treat them
☐ God is with you and loves you

PRAY

'Our Father, which art in heaven...'

HYMN OR SONG

'In heavenly love abiding'
(CD, *Words of peace*, track 27)

'TO HIM WHO IS ABLE...'

CUES AND CLUES

Some of the following might help as you read today's verses from the Bible and pray.

Pictures
A person walking with a stick; a king on a throne.

Objects
A walking stick or frame.

PRAYER

Lord God, we praise you for your care and love. You are with us as we walk through life, and for always. *Amen.*

READING Jude 24,25

To him who is able to keep you from falling and to present you before his glorious presence without fault and with great joy – to the only God our Saviour be glory, majesty, power and authority, through Jesus Christ our Lord, before all ages, now and for evermore! Amen.
Jude 24,25

TALK ABOUT...
☐ Falling and being helped up by others
☐ Jesus takes care of us
☐ Thanking God for his goodness
☐ Eternal life with God, heaven

PRAY
'Our Father, which art in heaven...'

HYMN OR SONG
'Jesus, the very thought of thee'
(CD, *Words of peace*, track 28)

29

'HERE I AM...'

CUES AND CLUES

Some of the following might help as you read today's verses from the Bible and pray.

Pictures
The Light of the World by Holman Hunt.

Objects
A door knocker or doorbell.

PRAYER
Lord Jesus, help us to hear your voice and welcome you into our lives today. *Amen.*

READING Revelation 3:20

Here I am! I stand at the door and knock. If anyone hears my voice and opens the door, I will come in and eat with him, and he with me.
Revelation 3:20

TALK ABOUT...
☐ Different kinds of doors, door knockers, doorbells
☐ Reminiscences about guests coming to visit
☐ Jesus wants to be part of our lives today

PRAY
'Our Father, which art in heaven...'

HYMN OR SONG
'Behold me standing at the door'
(CD, *Words of peace*, track 29)

NO MORE CRYING...

CUES AND CLUES

Some of the following might help as you read today's verses from the Bible and pray.

Pictures
A picture of someone being comforted or having tears wiped away.

Objects
A handkerchief (to suggest the drying of tears).

PRAYER
Father God, thank you that one day there will no more tears – and thank you for your presence and comfort with us today. *Amen.*

READING Revelation 21:1–4

Then I saw a new heaven and a new earth ... and God himself will be with them and be their God. He will wipe every tear from their eyes. There will be no more death or mourning or crying or pain, for the old order of things has passed away.
Revelation 21:1,3,4

TALK ABOUT...
☐ Being comforted
☐ Heaven – what it will be like
☐ All our troubles will be gone
☐ God will be with us, caring and providing for us

PRAY
'Our Father, which art in heaven...'

HYMN OR SONG
'Steal away to Jesus'
(CD, *Words of peace,* track 30)

THE RIVER
OF LIFE

CUES AND CLUES

Some of the following might help as you read today's verses from the Bible and pray.

Pictures
Streams, rivers, water; a beautiful city with trees, fountains and a river.

Objects
A jug of cold water and glasses; a leafy plant.

To do
Have a drink of water.

PRAYER
Lord God, our Saviour and King, we praise you for your promises of life with you for ever. *Amen.*

READING Revelation 22:1–5

Then the angel showed me the river of the water of life, as clear as crystal, flowing from the throne of God and of the Lamb ... On each side of the river stood the tree of life ... And the leaves of the tree are for the healing of the nations.
Revelation 22:1,2

TALK ABOUT...
☐ Rivers and streams – any favourites
☐ Swimming in rivers; drinking cold, fresh water when you're thirsty
☐ God gives us all we need for life
☐ God is King and will make everything right
☐ God's people will be with him for ever

PRAY
'Our Father, which art in heaven...'

HYMN OR SONG
'Crown him with many crowns'
(CD, *Words of peace*, track 31)

FURTHER
RESOURCES

Worship with people with dementia

'Holy, Holy, Holy': The church's ministry with people with dementia by Jackie Treetops, available from Faith in Elderly People (contact details, page 46).

The Wells of Life: Moments of worship with people with dementia by Gaynor Hammond and Jackie Treetops, available from Faith in Elderly People (contact details, page 46).

Worship for People with Dementia, a booklet based on material by Margaret Goodall, Gaynor Hammond and Laraine Moffitt, available from MHA (contact details, page 46).

Hymns and songs

There are several good websites where you can find words and music for hymns and songs. Try: www.cyberhymnal.org

Memory and reminiscence

Memories are Made of This: Reminiscence activities for person-centred care by Julie Heathcote, available from Alzheimer's Society (contact details, page 46).

The Memory Box by Gaynor Hammond, available from Faith in Elderly People (contact details, page 46).

Pictures to Share These books of pictures are ideal for sharing with people with dementia. Themes covered in the titles include: Childhood, Funny Old World, In the Garden, Beside the Seaside, A Sporting Life, The Countryside, A Woman's Work, Travelling, Shopping, Pets. Available from: www.picturestoshare.co.uk

For carers and churches

In a Strange Land: People with dementia and the church by Malcolm Goldsmith, available from 4M Publications: www.4mpublications.co.uk; or: www.amazon.co.uk

USEFUL
CONTACT DETAILS

MHA
Epworth House,
Stuart Street,
Derby DE1 2EQ

01332 296200
enquiries@mha.org.uk
www.mha.org.uk

**Christian Council
on Ageing**
info@ccoa.org.uk
www.ccoa.org.uk

Faith in Elderly People
Publications:
Gaynor Hammond
29 Silverdale Avenue,
Guiseley,
Leeds, LS20 8BD

01943 879320
gaynor.hammond@northern.org.uk

Alzheimer's Society
Devon House,
58 St Katharine's Way,
London E1W 1JX

+44 (0) 20 7423 3500
enquiries@alzheimers.org.uk
www.alzheimers.org.uk

BEING WITH GOD

A Bible and prayer guide
for people with dementia

OTHER TITLES AVAILABLE
IN THIS SERIES:

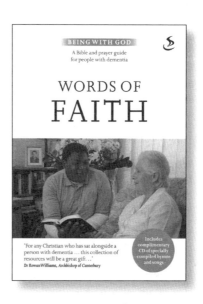

Words of hope

- Jesus – light and life
- Psalms – words of hope

ISBN 9781844275205

Words of faith

- Jesus – words and stories
- God's heroes – faithful lives

ISBN 9781844275212

£6.99 each

Available from your local **Christian bookshop**
from **www.scriptureunion.org.uk/shop**
or from Scripture Union Mail Order on **0845 07 06 006**

CD:
WORDS OF PEACE

Hymns and songs

1 'How great thou art'
2 'Count your blessings'
3 'Trust and obey'
4 'He who would valiant be'
5 'Up from the grave he arose'
6 'Silent night, holy night'
7 'O worship the Lord in the beauty of holiness'
8 'Be still my soul'
9 'The old rugged cross'
10 'What a friend we have in Jesus'
11 'Just a closer walk with thee'
12 'Breathe on me breath of God'
13 'Praise to the Holiest in the height'
14 'Blessed assurance, Jesus is mine'
15 'Dear Lord and Father of mankind'
16 'O Love that wilt not let me go'
17 'Sweet is the work, my God, my King'
18 'Love divine, all loves excelling'
19 'Give me joy in my heart…' ('peace', 'love')
20 'A wonderful Saviour is Jesus my Lord'
21 'Fight the good fight'
22 'All hail the power of Jesus' name'
23 'Jesus is the sweetest name I know'
24 'O happy day'
25 'Turn your eyes upon Jesus'
26 'Read your Bible, pray every day'
27 'In heavenly love abiding'
28 'Jesus, the very thought of thee'
29 'Behold me standing at the door'
30 'Steal away to Jesus'
31 'Crown him with many crowns'

Acknowledgements:
Original recordings made at Frog Studios, Cheshire and on location by **Gordon Lorenz**.

Featuring...
Vocalists: Ian Wallace, Jean Barrowman, Valerie Monese, Hero Douglas, John Delbridge.
Choirs: St George's Chapel Choir, Windsor Castle; Treorchy Male Voice Choir; The Choir of Guildford Cathedral; The Massed Choirs of Yorkshire; The Castleford Singers; The Gordon Lorenz Singers; Colwyn Bay Children's Choir.
Musicians: The Brighouse and Rastrick Brass Band, Matthew Freeman, Steve Millington, Barry Thompson

Engineers: Mark Walker and Richard Scott.

Mastered at RAS Studios, Manchester. All recordings produced by **Gordon Lorenz**.